IMAGES OF ENGLAND

BASINGSTOKE

T OF BERK

Newton
Knight Br
to Newbury
Anborn R.
Pamber For.
Silchester
Stratf
M
Cler ewood
Clere
ghclere
Wulferton
b Tadley
Baghurst
Bramley
Mattingle
Hertley w
Kingscler
a
Pam-ber
Sherfield
Sidmonton
E
Skerwes
4
Lichfield
G
Shernborn
Newnham
K
averstoke
7
Wotton
Basing
Polham
10
Okeley
C Okely
4
Dogm
O diam
Dean
Be
F
Sutto
10
Stephen
ton
Ilsfield
Farleigh
Harcote
Wanboro
Foyl
8
Dumer
I
Lasham
Alton
Michel
dever
Chilton
Bradley
c
R
S
Medsted
Abitching
Abbaston
burn
Arlington
Caston
7
Alesford
Bughton
8
Faringdon
Ropley
R ot herf
Cheryton
V

IMAGES OF ENGLAND

BASINGSTOKE

MALCOLM PARKER

TEMPUS

Frontispiece: Hermann Moll, a Dutchman and a leading geographer of his day produced this map in 1724 as part of his atlas *New Description of England and Wales.* The dotted lines signify hundreds or county divisions and the mileage is shown between destinations.

Then of a similar size as Whitchurch or Alresford, Basingstoke's position at a major junction between turnpike routes would prove significant as land transport grew in importance during the twentieth century.

First published 2007

Tempus Publishing Limited
The Mill, Brimscombe Port,
Stroud, Gloucestershire, GL5 2QG
www.tempus-publishing.com

British Library Cataloguing in Publication Data.
A catalogue record for this book is available from the British Library.

ISBN 978 07524 3082 9

Typesetting and origination by Tempus Publishing Limited.
Printed in Great Britain.

Contents

	Acknowledgements	6
	Introduction	6
one	'A Good Market Town'	9
two	'Fallen into Manufacture'	15
three	Days of Empire	35
four	The Edwardians	55
five	The Great War	71
six	A Brief Intermission	81
seven	Second World War	97
eight	Post-War Redevelopment	103

Acknowledgements

I should like to thank Sue Tapliss and the staff of the Willis Museum, Basingstoke for their help and support during this book's development, Basingstoke Library and Hampshire Record Office who have helped with information, Hampshire County Museums Service for permission to reproduce the majority of photographs in this book, and Wendy Bowen for her assistance in helping me to find my way around the archives. The *Basingstoke Gazette* for permission to reproduce some quotes and photographs and the *Hampshire Magazine* for permission to reproduce the quote from John Arlott.

I am also grateful to the following for permission to use their photographs: G.E. Adnams, S.C. Brown, David Bearne and Paul and Ursula Jeffree.

I would also thank Lindsay Beaton, Michael Stockwell and Phoebe Roman without whose help and encouragement this book would never have been possible.

This book owes a great debt to the people of Basingstoke who have over the years taken and very generously donated their photographs to the Willis Museum and to the Hampshire County Museums Service.

Thank You.

Introduction

'Basingstoke – A thriving Hampshire town'

The focus of this book is the town of Basingstoke as it was before 1967. From almost every perspective, the town as it stands today is fundamentally a different place to the town as it was then. Not that what has happened since 1967 is unimportant or uninteresting, indeed this may be the most important time in the town's history. According to published statistics, its people are now generally better educated, better housed, better fed, longer lived, more likely to be working and more affluent than at any other time in its history and there are also far more of them with the current estimate for 2006 showing just under 80,500 people resident in the town and just under 157,000 in the borough of Basingstoke and Deane. This compares with 52,000 for the town and almost 104,000 for the borough in 1971.

In these historic times for the town, we can boast a number of upcoming athletes like 400m runner Robin Tobin or tennis player Josh Goodall. We can brag that the highly respected *Sunday Times* art critic Waldemar Januszczak was born in Basingstoke, as was film star Elizabeth Hurley, *Dirty Pretty Things* frontman Carl Barât and world-ranked pool player Kim 'The Cooler' Shaw. We can even boast a *Playboy* model in the shape of Rachel Cole.

That said, it's important we don't take ourselves too seriously; after all we were unabashed hosts to two comedy films in the 1930s and 1940s, we have a street apparently renamed after a spelling mistake – oats the crop being so repeatedly pronounced 'woats' when said in its proper 'ampshire accent, that in consequence Oat Street officially became Wote Street at some time in the 1850s after a long history of frequent misspellings. We have Gilbert and Sullivan using the word 'Basingstoke' to temper the insane ravings of Mad Margaret in *Ruddigore* and even that inestimable chap in English comedy writing, Bertie Wooster, reminiscing fondly about his visits here as a child in P.G. Wodehouse's book *The Mating Season*.

This book is a far from a comprehensive history – the last attempt at that was published in 1889 by Francis Baigent, a Winchester antiquary and Dr James Millard, vicar of Basingstoke and former headmaster of Magdalen College Oxford. It ran to over 750 pages and even then had no photographs, covered little in the way of social history or the local dialect and could tell us nothing at all of what everyday folk were thinking. My book is simply a series of illustrations, a brief guide with the accompaniment of photographs through some celebrated and hopefully interesting points in the town's history and development.

Mankind wandered into this fertile land at the head of the River Loddon long before the days of recorded history. Scattered finds covering an extensive period from the Old Stone Age to the Roman abound, and there is evidence of numerous pre-Domesday settlements.

Anglo-Saxon settlements leave little in the way of tangible artefacts and unfortunately, and unforgivably from a historical perspective, much of the redevelopment that took place in the town centre in 1967 was without any regard to archaeological investigation. The deep excavations and wholesale destruction carried out then, leave an enormous gap in accurately plotting a major part of the town's development and this loss can never be filled. Thankfully in recent years a more enlightened approach has been taken, allowing major studies to take place of the deserted medieval village of Hatch (now Hatch Warren), an Anglo-Saxon site in Riverdene and the high status Middle-Saxon site at Cowdrey's Down, all before building commenced.

The earliest recorded reference to the area comes in the *Anglo-Saxon Chronicles* which tell of The Battle of Basengum that took place in the year 871 between the Danes and King Æthelred. To date, there is no archaeological evidence to determine precisely the location of this battle. Local legend and supposition suggests the battle took place near Basing and that the dead were buried at Lychpit. This may well be true, but equally what is now Basingstoke could have been the site of the battle and the assumed Anglo-Saxon burial ground at the Liten perhaps a little more significant than was previously thought.

Unpicking the precise relationship between Basingstoke and Basing in the Anglo-Saxon period is a subject worthy of more academic study but it appears that Basengum could have been a general term for the area until it became important to distinguish between its two primary settlements.

By the time of the survey for the Domesday Book in 1086, Basingstoke (*Basingestoch*) and Basing (*Basinges*) are given separate listings and the distinction is clear. Some debate remains, however, about the precise location of the Anglo-Saxon church, listed separately in the book as in the Basingstoke Hundred, but of which no trace is believed to remain today. This could be St Mary's in Basing or it may be what is now St Stephen's chapel in St Michael's church, the ancient south and east walls of which bear faint scars of filled-in windows and a doorway, and again, a detailed investigation of such features is long overdue.

The Domesday survey is also our first reference to the market in Basingstoke, one of only a handful recorded at that time in what would go on to become Hampshire. The market would remain, for the next 800 years at least, the fundamental heart and soul of the town.

The earliest intimation of any sort of manufacturing appears in 1273, when Basingstoke merchant John Finian was given a licence to export wool. Woollen goods, cloth, corn, gloves, leather, barley and malting are all noted at various times through the years as being important to the town's economy. Unlike nearby Alresford, Farnham or Winchester however, Basingstoke's merchants and manufacturers do not appear to have achieved any significant commercial success until the twentieth century and because of this, many of the buildings of Basingstoke appear to have remained on the whole modest and functional rather than grand and ostentatious. This is not to say that Basingstoke was unimportant in earlier times, simply that the wholesale redevelopment of many towns in the 1960s was rather more forgiving towards the legacy of Classical and Georgian architecture that such commercial booms had helped to create, rather than to the buildings of the later service and industrial era.

Fire may have been a significant factor in curtailing entrepreneurial ambition over the years, with major fires recorded in 1392, 1601 and 1656, although they in themselves are not unusual. As well as the economic setbacks that fires always produce, these did bring an end to the erection of low cost timber-framed buildings with thatched roofs. The very old town buildings that survived were often 'modernised' rather than demolished and replaced, and again such thrift was brutally punished in the 1960s when only intact and unchanged exteriors were deemed worthy of preservation.

Basingstoke's original street patterns were becoming well established by the fifteenth century and while the overall area of the town changed very little for the next 500 years, what were large gardens or agricultural plots, between the shops and houses that lined the street fronts, were gradually encroached upon through the nineteenth century. Storerooms, outbuildings and workshops gradually filled the gaps, until by the twentieth century – had they all been the same height it would almost have been possible to walk from one end of the town to the other directly across the rooftops. The only remaining viewpoint in the town centre, to give a hint of what it looked like then, is the view from the library balcony towards Cross Street and Church Street.

The town has produced or played host to some important figures during its history, although not all are as widely acclaimed as they might be. Thomas Warton is celebrated as poet laureate, but perhaps deserves higher praise for his talents as an academic and researcher; indeed his brother and father might be said to have been equally noteworthy figures. John Arlott became famous as a charismatic cricket commentator, but his essays for the *Hampshire Magazine* and his other writings should not be overlooked. Harriot Stanton Blatch, one of the most important figures in the American Women's Rights movement, and as celebrated as Emmeline Pankhurst there, lived in Basingstoke for about twenty years. Finally Gilbert White, perhaps the greatest naturalist in British history received much of his early education here, even if he did admit to assisting other boys in the 'wanton destruction of the Holy Ghost Chapel.'

Pick up almost any Hampshire guide book from the 1950s or 1960s and it's clear that few outsiders could see anything notable about Basingstoke beyond the concentrated urbanity of the town; Pevsner's famous guide *The Buildings of England* is particularly damming. In truth, Victoriana was then heavily out of fashion and generally ignored, the streets of Basingstoke, though much widened, were woefully inadequate to cope with the ever-increasing traffic and much of the town centre was looking pretty shabby.

Basingstoke's redevelopment in the 1960s will always remain controversial, but many of the changes that came with it, particularly the loss of small independent shops and long-established businesses and the immeasurable change in society from one of generally respectful servitude to what some now regard as arrogant self-interest and self-obsession were symptomatic of changes to English society as a whole. Basingstoke changed monumentally, but so did the rest of the country. In the unlikely event that Basingstoke had remained untouched by developers, it is inconceivable that the small happy community that existed just after the war would have continued unchanged. Like a much-loved old coat, the town was worn at the seams, no longer fitted properly and had simply gone out of fashion, but when we look back we only tend to remember what it was like on the first day that we wore it and wish longingly that somehow we had managed to keep it.

In conclusion, try not to view these black and white photographs through rose-coloured spectacles. The community was more close-knit and trusting not simply because it was a lot smaller, but also because it needed to be; you were unlikely to get new neighbours, the only entertainment available was almost entirely communal and with no free health care, no state pension and very little in the way of financial flexibility, you needed all the friends you could get. Crime, violence, depression, drunkenness, litter and ignorance certainly did not begin in 1967 and then, like now, happiness was really all about your own state of mind.

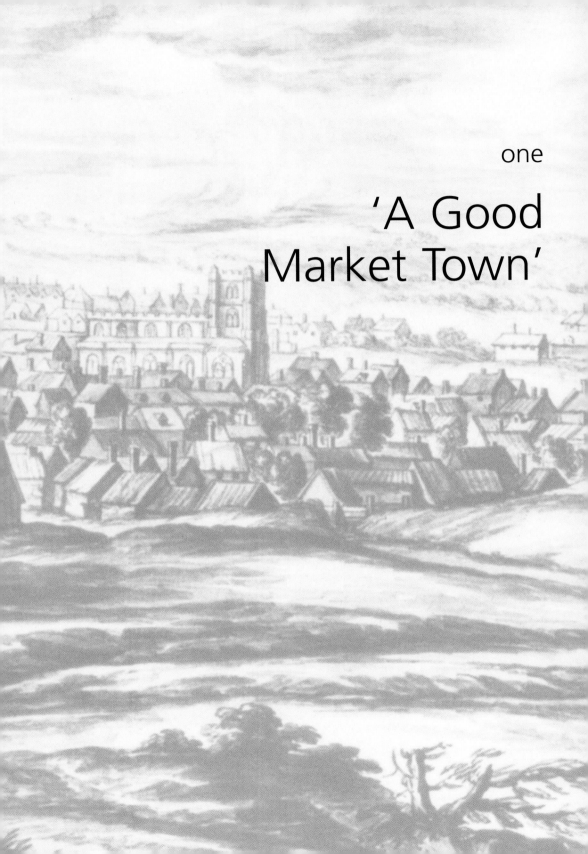

one

'A Good
Market Town'

Winklebury Ring, *c.* 1900. A defensive complex occupied between *c.* 600 and *c.*100 BC and perhaps one of the most tangible signs of early settlement in Basingstoke's immediate area. Neglected somewhat in recent years, a conservation group of local volunteers has now been formed to help maintain the site.

A speculative depiction of the Holy Ghost chapel in Tudor times painted in 1884 by Windover Workman. The early chapel to the rear is thought to have been completed around 1244 but should have a square tower to the left – the walls of which are the only part standing today. To the right Lord Sandys' chapel of the Holy Trinity was added in 1520 by which time the original chapel was being used as a school. This brick-built, stone-faced extension was renowned for its sumptuous interior decoration.

Above: Deane's Almshouses floodlit by gaslight in 1930. Sir James Deane founded these almshouses in 1607 but died before their completion. An elm referred to as 'the Great Tree' on a 1762 map and said to commemorate the Gunpowder Plot stood near the houses from 1605 to 1809.

Right: Sir Richard Aldworth, *c.* 1646. A wealthy merchant of London and Reading whose wife came from a prominent Basingstoke family. He bequeathed money (equivalent to over £2 million today) to found Blue Coat schools in Basingstoke and Reading and also to the original Blue Coat School at Christ's Hospital, London where he was a governor. His school in Basingstoke closed in 1879, but his name lives on at the Aldworth Science College in South Ham.

capella ruinosa SSpiritus apud **Basingstoke** .

Henrico Torkington de Surkeley ☗ mag.Ar.Tabula Votiva .

The chapel of the Holy Trinity in 1722. Vandalised by Cromwell's troops during the Civil War, a minor quibble over the cost of repairs in 1692 left the work undone and gave us the ruin much as we see it today.

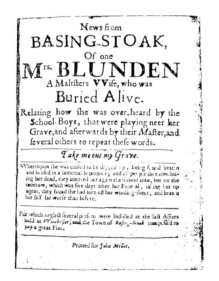

Left: In July 1674, a grave and unfortunate incident occurred, when Mrs Alice Blunden was unlucky enough to find herself buried in the Holy Ghost cemetery whilst she was only slightly dead.

A sensationalised account of the events of this case appeared in this pamphlet published in London shortly afterwards. A far less graphic account published in 1740 by the respected French anatomist Jacob Benignus Winsløw is probably somewhat closer to fact. What appears to have happened is that while her husband was away on business, Mrs Blunden (a reputed hypochondriac) felt ill, sending to the local pharmacist for a quantity of poppy water – an opium-based narcotic later known as laudanum – which she then proceeded to drink until she fell into a coma.

Such was her level of unconsciousness, and so crude the methods for determining death in those days that it was assumed that she had died. Then, because the weather was very hot, her funeral and subsequent burial took place very promptly.

Shortly afterwards, children who were playing in the burial ground reported to the local school master (their school house being in the cemetery grounds) that they had heard a noise apparently coming from her grave. This was dismissed at first, but as other children repeated these claims they were soon taken more seriously. Unfortunately by the time the grave could be reopened it was too late to do anything to revive the unfortunate Mrs Blunden. It was clear she had been buried alive but was now really dead for good! History does not record her gravestone epitaph, but I think it probably omitted the familiar 'Only Sleeping'.

An artist in the entourage of Cosmo III, Grand Duke of Tuscany, sketched the earliest known visual depiction of the town from the Liten in 1669. Engravings from this sketch were first published in 1821. This is a later, embellished version of the rather simplistic original engraving with a more accurate portrayal of the church.

Church Cottage, *c.* 1860. Despite its name and its situation behind St Michael's church, the cottage's direct connection with the church appears only to date from the eighteenth century. The earliest part of the building was built with timbers cut in 1527 and though its precise origins are uncertain, for many years it was owned and used by families connected with Basingstoke's cloth industry.

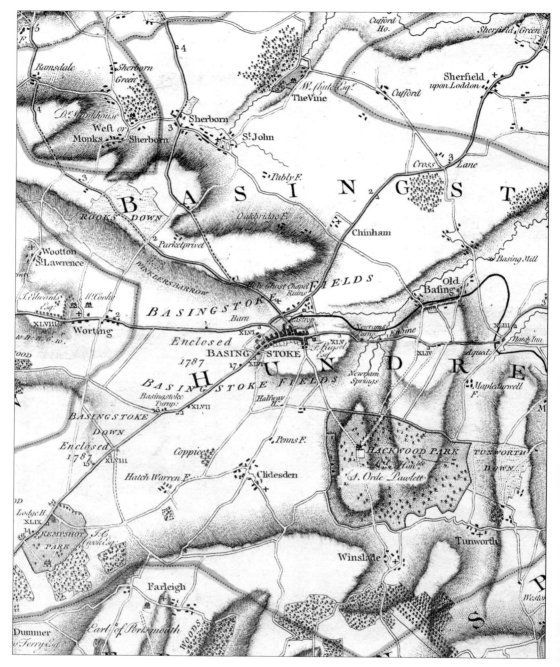

Thomas Milne surveyed this map between 1788 and 1790 and added a rather simplified version of the final stages of the route of the Basingstoke Canal – then nearing completion – into Basingstoke. At that time the intention was to link this canal with the Andover Canal to Southampton, but the difficulties with this and with successive alternatives proved insurmountable and doomed what was always a rather optimistic endeavour to becoming little more than a white elephant until its true value and potential as a public amenity was recognised in the 1960s.

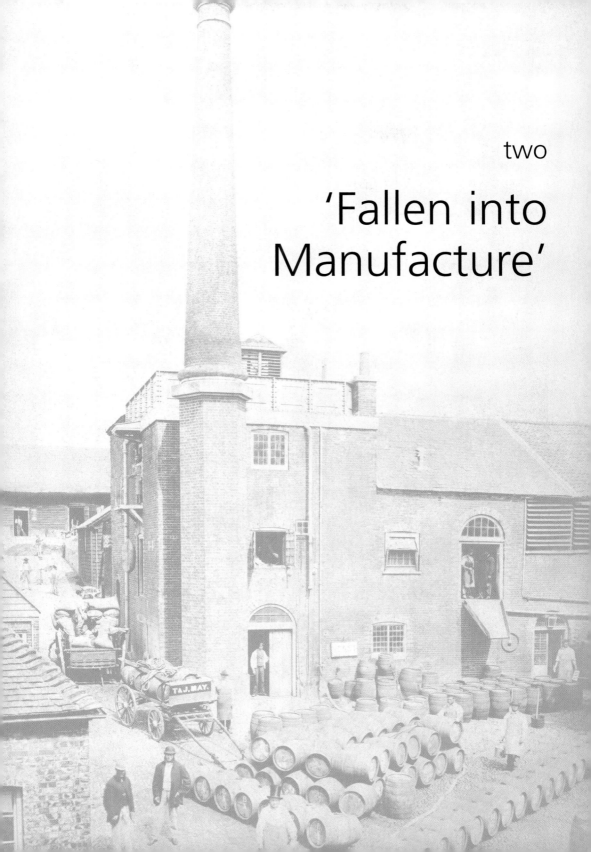

two

'Fallen into
Manufacture'

Toll Gate by H.C. Andrews, Flaxfield College, Basingstoke, *c.* 1880. In the agricultural era of the eighteenth century, the financial benefits to the town from Turnpikes were relatively minor. As road transport increased in importance in the twentieth century however, these crucial long-established pathways gave Basingstoke a significant commercial advantage from which the town continues to profit.

The Angel, an engraved billhead from 1863. The railway arrived in Basingstoke in 1839 and quickly bought real economic benefits with its speed and general reduction of transport costs. It spelt the end for many large inns like the Angel, which were dependent on long-distance road traffic. The Angel closed in 1866.

Robert Cottle's shop in Winchester Street from an 1836 billhead. Five times mayor of the town, Cottle was appointed postmaster in 1814 and his postbox – one of the oldest surviving in the country – can still be seen in the Willis Museum. As a printer he published a number of fine engravings of town buildings. His shop is still largely recognisable today.

A delightful handbill surviving from 1856 with many events surely long overdue for revival. Does anyone know the rules for Jingling matches? The Fair Close is now the site of Fairfields School.

RUSTIC AMUSEMENTS
IN THE FAIR-CLOSE,
For the 29th MAY, 1856,

TO COMMENCE WITH

A grand WHEELBARROW RACE, in Heats, 12 Competitors, blindfolded, with a "Look-out Man" in each Barrow, the Winner to receive 10s. and the Second, 5s.

A RACE to be contended for by 20 Boys, between 12 and 14 Years of Age, the Winner to receive a NEW CAP, value 2s. 6d.

JUMPING in SACKS, between 12 men, the Winner to be entitled to 7s. 6d. the second, 3s. 6d.

A HURDLE RACE, out and home, between 12, over 6 flights of Hurdles, the Winner to be entitled to 5s the second 2s. 6d.

DITTO ditto, the Winners of the former to be excluded.

A GRAND JINGLING MATCH for 5s. to be open for all ages and ranks to compete for. time, 10 minutes.

DITTO, ditto for BOYS under 14 years of age. Prize 2s. 6d.

A HAT RACE, value 7s. 6d. between 20, for all above 16 Years of Age

A CAP RACE for BOYS between 8 and 10.

CLIMBING the GREASY POLE, with LEGS of MUTTON attached, to commence at 6 o'Clock.

Any of the above Games will be repeated, or others added, at the Discretion of the Committee of Management, whose decision, if any disputes arise, shall be final.

All Competitors to give in their Names at the Committees' Tent before 5 o'Clock.

The Fireworks to commence at NINE o'Clock.

BY ORDER OF THE COMMITTEE OF MANAGEMENT.

R. Cottle, Printer.

Junction of London Street and the Market Place by G. Woodman, 1871. Woodman was born in Basingstoke in the 1850s and his recollections, published in the *Hants and Berks Gazette* in the 1920s, provide a vivid illustration of the town as it was during the mid-nineteenth century.

The Holy Ghost chapel, *c.* 1830. An engraving by G.F. Prosser showing the Free School building on the left. In 1818, it is said that an over-enthusiastic schoolmaster decided to complete the destruction of the chapel remains, but was fortunately restrained by townsfolk.

A MEMORY of 1870 BY N.W. WOODCOCK

Above: Basingstoke's first Wesleyan Methodist chapel was in this old granary in Potter's Lane. The steps to the front door were eventually pulled up during services as young boys had discovered what fun could be had by removing them. Later the building was rebuilt as the British Workman Tea Rooms.

Right: John Hall of Church Street, *c.* 1860. Mr Hall, a blacksmith, was born in Potter's Lane in 1822 and is remarkable in that while lots of early portrait photographs of 'ordinary' folk survive, very few tell us who the sitter was or where they lived. If you are lucky enough to possess any early photographs of members of your family, do please take steps to identify them before such invaluable information is lost.

Left: The Holy Ghost or Free School building photographed shortly before its demolition, around 1857 and possibly the oldest known photograph taken in the town. At the time of its demolition, the sale of a field know as Maiden Acre for a new cemetery just north of where it stood caused a near riot when it was wrongly believed that the land was public property held only for the school.

Below: Chapel Street, *c.* 1846. From a travelling chart to the South Western Railway. In 1848, two years after this publication, a second completely independent railway station was opened in the town, directly alongside the first, bringing the Great Western Railway line from Reading.

WORTING CHURCH.

Above: Worting church, *c.* 1800. Rebuilt after an enormous fire in the village in May 1655, St Thomas of Canterbury remained largely unchanged until 1847-53 when it was 'improved' and enlarged at a cost of £2,300.

Right: Mayor Charles Webb, local dignitaries and throngs of spectators await the arrival of the Prince and Princess of Wales at Basingstoke Station in 1863. Though the royal party did not disembark, the train paused long enough to allow an official presentation of congratulations on the couple's marriage and major celebrations followed around the town. *The Times* commented witheringly, 'The Royal Train stopped at Basingstoke to take on water'.

Above and below: Initially goods were transferred from rail to road without any sophistication. Warehousing was built around 1850 by merchants Richard Wallis in Bunnian Place and Henry Jesse in Chapel Street to transfer goods from rail to road level and vice versa. Both warehouses were demolished in 1904 when the railway was widened.

Above: James Butler's smithy beside the Foresters Arms in Cambridge Terrace, *c.* 1880. The man with the watch chain is said to be Frederick Lodder, a watchmaker from Winchester Street.

Right: The Town Hall, *c.* 1870. Designed by Lewis. Wyatt and built in 1832 at a cost of £10,000. In 1865 the open Market Place on the ground floor was fully enclosed and the balcony and the seal of Basingstoke added to the frontage.

Above: London Street, 1862. A contemporary directory describes the roads of the period as 'good' though clearly this did not necessarily mean they were amenable to pedestrians. The ramshackle, jettied building on the left-hand side was the Fleur-de-lis, originally known as the Falcon where Oliver Cromwell lodged during the siege of Basing House.

Left: New Street and Winchester Street junction, *c.* 1860. The white building is Robert Meatyard's chemist shop with his assistant David Langden Bird in the doorway; the man in the top hat is said to be Robert Archer Davis, mayor of Basingstoke 1865-66. Amongst diverse products issued by Meatyard around this time were Jones' Prometheans & Lucifers for producing a light without a bottle, Roll Brimstone and Sulphur, the Vermifuge Electuary and Meatyard's own Camphoric Vegetable Tooth Powder.

Above: Sapp's chemist shop at the junction of London Street and the Market Place. Sapp came from Chichester, building up his trade with Mr Meatyard in the premises shown previously before establishing his own shop shown here in 1872.

Right: Sapp was equally prolific in the supply of patent and homoeopathic medicines, along with leeches, water beds and surgical appliances. Regrettably the formula for his exclusive Basingstoke Bouquet appears to have been lost when Mr Sapp died in 1886. His son, who was also named Arkas, went on to become a very well known local builder. The shop was then sold to H. Allen, another former mayor who built up a chain of chemists around Hampshire, which lasted until the 1950s.

Above: Winchester Street, 1862. Basingstoke's population in the 1860s was about the same as Overton's is today. About 40 per cent of the total labour force worked in agriculture although few would have a permanent job.

Left: William Willis's saddle, harness and string makers shop in Winchester Street, *c.* 1860. William was the grandfather of George Willis who would later help to found the town museum.

Right: On the opposite corner of New Street from Meatyard's chemists was the bootmakers shop of Walter Wyeth, seen here around 1880. Mr Wyeth is in the doorway next to Charles Myland, a town postman.

Below: Old 'Green', a market trader, with his vegetable cart, *c.* 1880. Mortimer Timson of Sarum Hill, one of the town's pioneer photographers, took this photograph.

Cross Street, *c.* 1860. The building on the right is the Blue Coat and National School, the charity boarding school founded by Richard Aldworth; its façade dates from 1718 though the building itself was much earlier.

Wote Street, *c.* 1860. William Seymour's premises stood where the bottom of Wote Street ends today. He was one of the town's last curriers, an ancient craft that with hard work, skill and special tools, transformed tanned leather into a pliant workable material. He was mayor in 1860–61.

The British School, Sarum Hill, *c.* 1875. Before the Education Act of 1870, schooling for the masses was primarily concerned with moral discipline and social subordination rather than individual advancement, in spite of which it still could meet with opposition. 'When they grow up we will get no work out of them', one observer is reported to have said when this school opened in 1841.

Flaxfield College, Flaxfield Road, *c.* 1880. Dr Arthur Greenwood – with moustache – was head of this boarding and preparatory school for boys near Flaxfield House. Founded around 1818 by John Fooks, the college was one of several private schools in the town. It appears to have closed around the time of the Education Act of 1902.

Above: Goat Lane and Wote Street junction, *c.* 1880. Edwin Glanville came from Oxfordshire and had lived in New Zealand for a time before setting up shop in Basingstoke where he stayed for twenty years and had three children. He moved to Reigate around 1899.

Left: George Willis's shop, Wote Street, *c.* 1880. Having served an apprenticeship with Frederick Lodder in Winchester Street, George Willis Snr opened this first shop near to Goat Lane in 1878. In 1881 he moved the business to larger premises at the top of Wote Street, where following a stroke his son took over from him in 1900.

May's Brewery, Brook Street, *c.* 1860. The Mays came from a wealthy family of yeoman and gentlemen farmers and established what became Basingstoke's biggest brewery in 1750. A major fire in 1870 destroyed the original malthouse – melted lead and grain from which can still be seen in the Willis Museum. The business proved very lucrative and provided employment for many in the town until its decline in the 1930s and ultimate closure in 1950. The 'T' and 'J' on the wagons stand for Thomas and John, the third generation of Mays to manage the business.

North Hants Iron Works, junction of Reading Road and Station Hill, *c.* 1862. Arthur Wallis and Charles Haslam came together around 1856 and were joined by Charles Steevens about ten years later. Haslam retired in 1869 and, as Wallis & Steevens, the company progressed from the manufacture of agricultural implements to portable steam engines with which to power them.

Wallis and Haslam employees in 1865. At this time Saturday was still a normal workday and it was only following the Newcastle Engineers strike of 1871 that the normal working week – excluding break times – was reduced from sixty to fifty-four hours.

St Michael's church, *c.* 1870. The typical Victorian makeover given to St Michaels by architect John Clacy was commendably conservative with regard to its exterior which was crowned by a 'Stately diadem of pinnacled turrets' added as the conclusion of this work between 1865-78.

The rectory and vicar's meadow, *c.* 1870. From a series of early commercial photographs taken by Alfred Seeley of Richmond. It is generally said that the rectory was built around 1773 although the parsonage, which preceded it, appears to have been very similar. It was bought by the council in 1969 and renamed Chute House in honour of Canon Anthony Chute, the vicar of St Michaels between 1936 and 1958. This idyllic photograph contrasts sharply with comments made by vicar J.E. Millard around this time, 'Two streams unite in the rectory grounds, their "sweetness" polluted by the sewage of the town for which this river is now the principle channel'.

VIEW OF
The Interior of S. MICHAEL'S CHURCH Basingstoke.
As it appeared in the Year 1840.

Above and left: St Michael's church interior by (*left*), E. Dukes, 1840 and (*above*), by A.H. Dykes, 1912. Anglican church services altered fundamentally after the 1840s, demanding a comprehensive rearrangement of church interiors. A wealth of fixtures and fittings built up over the preceding three centuries were removed to give a far less cosy pseudo-medieval style more conducive to the order and dignity of the new proceedings. St Michael's wonderful Jacobean pulpit and fifteenth-century font were moved to St Mary's, Old Basing, but much else was simply discarded. On the plus side, heating and lighting were added, allowing evening services to be held. Fortunately the wonderful, painted Royal Arms of Elizabeth I, James I and William III were all preserved.

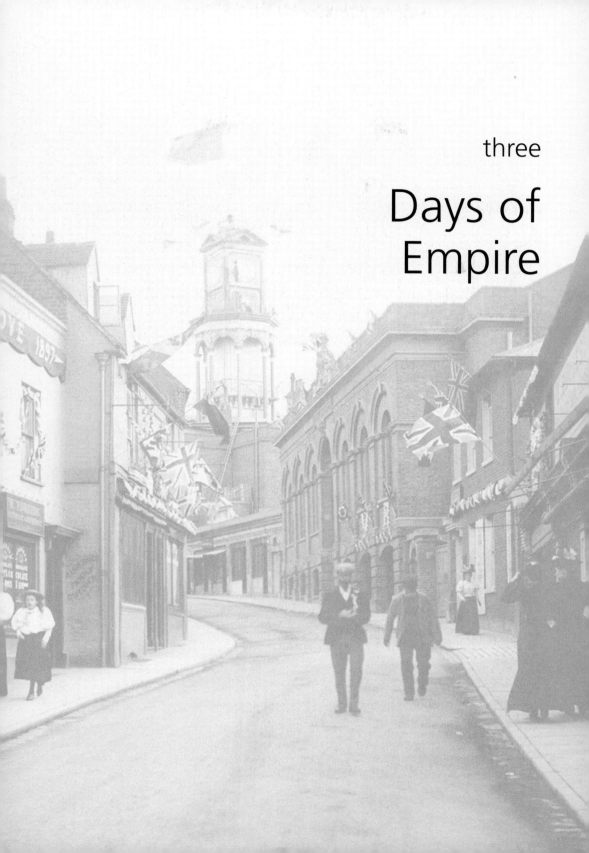

three

Days of Empire

Davis & Stephens Timber Yard, Chapel Hill, *c.* 1870. Established in an area known as Moon Close, Robert Davis and Gerrald Stephens were another merchant partnership to prosper from the coming of the railway. Their yard was eventually sold to the Southampton-based company Tagart, Morgan & Coles who ran it until the 1970s. In the background is one of the two mortuary chapels, built along with a cemetery gatehouse in the new cemetery between 1857-58. They were designed by Poulton & Woodman of Reading, but fell out of use when the cemetery closed for burials after the First World War. Both chapels were demolished – not without protest – in the 1950s and only the gatehouse remains.

Basingstoke from the Liten, *c.* 1880. One of the best views across Basingstoke, sketched by J.M.W. Turner in 1811, was interrupted when the railway arrived, gradually disappearing when the station expanded in the 1890s before being finally lost altogether when the line was doubled and the station rebuilt in 1904.

Basingstoke policemen, 1889. From left to right, back row: Sgt William Todd and constables, ? Mears, ? Astridge, Charles Treagus. Front row: James White, Clement Burden, James Hibberd.

Reading Road, c. 1895. Directly opposite the Waggon & Horses public house and behind what were known as 'the Little Almshouses' on the left, the Salvation Army built its front line barracks in 1883. In 1881 fighting the good fight became literal for the army in Basingstoke where their initially untempered, dogmatical evangelism led to a reading of the Riot Act and questions in the House of Commons.

London Road junction with Redbridge Lane, *c.* 1910. The telegraph had arrived in Basingstoke shortly after the railway, initially following the railway lines. After the telephone was developed in the 1880s the network of wires expanded rapidly and enormous telegraph poles like the ones in this photograph soon became a familiar sight. Basingstoke railway station was telephone number one.

Tyrrell's Grocery store, *c.* 1890. Alfred Tyrrell took over the grocery store on the corner of the Market Place, *c.*1865. The shop was extended in the 1890s under the ownership of his relative William Tyrrell and briefly became the Labour Exchange before its demolition in the 1920s.

Above: Basingstoke Volunteer Fire Brigade, Wote Street, 1887. The town's 'large' engine with Superintendent John Burgess Soper – with white beard – in the driving seat. Fire appliances including this Hadley, Simpkin and Lott pump were centralised at the Corn Exchange in 1869 when the volunteer brigade was organised, having been stored previously near the church and town hall.

Right: James Smith, *c.* 1890. Mr Smith was born in Basingstoke in 1792, and in 1817 stood guard over Napoleon at St Helena. In 1846 he became postman for Dummer and North Waltham. He was residing in Hackwood Road when he died in 1893 aged 102 and thousands were reported to have attended his funeral.

This photograph was labelled 'Basingstoke School Teachers', though it may actually be members of the Church of England Temperance Society, c. 1880. From left to right, back row: Mr R.J. Moth, Miss Elizabeth Kirk, Mr Skinner, Mrs Skinner, Miss Redgrove, Mr Skinner Jnr. Front row: Miss C.A. Hunt, Miss Goddard, Dr James Elwin Millard, Miss Isabella Coleman, Miss J. Moore. The fierce-looking Miss Coleman was a much-loved head of infants at the Basingstoke Board School.

The 'big' schoolroom, Queen Mary's School, Worting Road, c. 1890. The Holy Ghost School was renamed Queen Mary's when it moved to Worting Road in 1855. The school subsequently moved to Vyne Road in 1940 where in 1972 it was merged with Charles Chute Secondary Modern and renamed The Vyne Community School.

William Seal's shop, Wote Street, *c.* 1895. In 1860, William's father opened a fishmongers shop, also in Wote Street somewhere near Goat Lane. William – in the doorway – took over the Lesser Market shop after his elder brother Edward, who had opened it, died in 1883.

Joice's Coachbuilders, Windover Street, *c.* 1897. From left to right: Charlie Waters (blacksmith's viceman), Jack Waters (groom), Ernest? Beazley (painter), 'Bimbo' Watts (painter), Joe Hewitt (bodymaker), John Myland (wheeler), Richard? Musslewhite (bodymaker), Arnold Joice (bodymaker), Percy Oliver (bodymaker), Walter Arnold (foreman), Walter Woods (painter), Joe Beacon (painter), Harry Brown (blacksmith), Tom Armstrong (blacksmith's striker), 'Doctor' Watts (trimmer), George Hill (painter).

Above: The Market Place, *c.* 1900. Invented in 1839, the bicycle became very popular as road surfaces improved and commercial manufacture began in the 1860s. Nevertheless, the dictates of women's fashion meant specialised engineering was required and the ladies' bicycle did not appear until the 1880s.

Right: Mr A. Hailstone, secretary of Basingstoke's first cycling club with his club racer, *c.* 1880. The Penny Farthing style of bicycle was a popular but perilous solution to going faster until gears were perfected in the 1880s.

Opposite: Unrecorded festivities in the Market Place, *c.*1895.

Above: Smith Brother's grocery shop, No. 40 Wote Street, *c.* 1880. From left to right: J. Stevens, Adnams, Griffin, Horner, J. Drummond, S. Rodgers, W. Hailstone. Opened by William Smith in the 1840s, Smith's main business developed as agricultural merchants and their warehouse near the station was a familiar landmark in the 1950s and 1960s.

Left: Joseph Gripper's grocery shop, No. 28 Wote Street, *c.* 1900. This eighteenth-century shop, which can also be seen on the earlier photograph of Seymour's Curriers, would later be modified to become part of the Forrest Stores chain before its demolition in the 1960s. Prior to Mr Gripper taking over, Edwin Glanville had run the shop after he moved from the shop at the junction with Goat Lane. Joseph Gripper joined forces with Walter Smith around 1902 to form Smith & Gripper and they were later joined by Mr Tyrrell from the Market Place as the business of retail grocery evolved.

Above: Rear yard of William Cannon's butchers No. 5 London Street, *c.* 1895. It is currently the site of the post office. From left to right: Will Cannon (Jnr), John Cannon, Miss Joice, Willie Cannon, Mary Cannon, 'Frisco' Phillips. William Cannon made national headlines when as mayor he was barred from St Michael's church by the then vicar. The purpose of the strange carriage is unrecorded.

Right: Work begins on what will be Colebrook & Co.'s Fishmongers Shop, Market Place, *c.* 1902. The delightfully flamboyant building alongside was demolished in the 1930s.

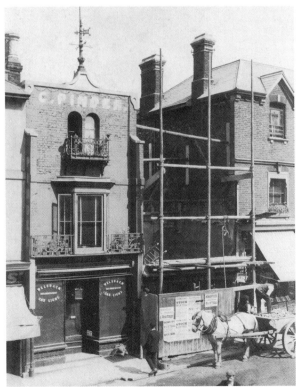

Wote Street, 1897. As two workers scale the heights of Lt-Col. May's Town Hall clock tower, passers-by stroll nonchalantly past without a glance. Perhaps like many others since, they're pondering if the tower really is a gesture of celebration for Queen Victoria or simply a mark of self-veneration.

Postmen, Wote Street, c. 1885. The post office moved to Wote Street in 1863, but the introduction of parcel post in 1883 required larger premises. Joseph Tigwell built these in that year opposite the old site, with the new post office on the right in this photograph and the sorting office through the arch. Tigwell's son took over the building when the post office moved on to New Street in the 1920s.

Hampshire County Council Farriery Class, Wheatsheaf Yard, *c.* 1895. From left to right: –?–, John Lansley, Arthur Toomer, –?–, William Coston, –?–, J.A. Viney. Coston was the landlord of the Wheatsheaf at this time.

Employees of Frederick Blunden's Wote Street Brewery, *c.* 1875. Blunden built up a meagre empire as a wine and spirit merchant in the 1850s, briefly taking over this brewery at its height. It proved a step too far, however, and he sold it again in 1878. The site is now buried somewhere beneath Debenhams.

Basingstoke Steam Laundry staff (and horses), Basing Road, *c.* 1895. Established in 1879. The 'steam' denoted a steam engine to power the machinery rather than steam being used directly to clean the clothes. The company initiated public baths off Wote Street but appears to have left this project at an early stage and the baths provided the foundation for one of Basingstoke's first cinemas, The Electric Theatre, which opened in 1910.

Winchester Street from the Market Place, *c.* 1880. Posters from Simmons & Sons on the Georgian bow-fronted shop advertise its sale, which would become home to Freeman, Hardy & Willis for many years. Sadly the bow windows are long gone, but otherwise these premises remain much the same today.

The Stag and Hounds Public House, Winchester Road, *c.* 1900. The Stag and Hounds dates back at least as far as 1826 and depending on which source you read is either on the site of, or was previously known as The Ship. Now very much extended, it has become a Harvester Restaurant.

The Swan Inn, No. 47 Wote Street, *c.* 1905. The Swan opened in the 1860s and this was taken shortly before its closure. It was briefly used as offices for the Basingstoke Char-à-banc & Motor Co. before being redeveloped in the 1930s.

Basingstoke Gas Works around 1900, which opened in late 1834. Gas was produced by heating coal, and then stored in large metal tanks before being distributed through underground pipes around the town. Initially lampposts were few and far between and even by 1851 there were only sixty-six for the whole town.

Basingstoke Gas Co. employees, Basingstoke Gas Works, *c.* 1894. By the 1850s gas was being used for cooking and lighting – at least in the homes that could afford it – and the gas works were enlarged several times to meet demand. Chief engineer William Higgs is seated centre front with his young son Herbert on his right who went on to become managing director in the 1930s.

Park Prewett Farm, *c.* 1895. Purchased along with 300 acres of land in 1900 as the site for The Basingstoke Asylum, work only got as far as planting the landmark belt of trees as a windbreak before being halted for ten years. Work resumed in 1913 and Park Prewett Mental Hospital finally opened in 1921. The farm remained operational until the 1990s.

Common keeper's cottage, Basingstoke Common, *c.* 1900. It was accessed via a lane known as The Pipes. If you drive east towards the Black Dam roundabout along Ringway South, near where you pass beneath the road bridge, this is roughly the view you would have got a century ago.

Wallis & Steevens, Top Shed, Station Hill, *c.* 1892. The company began the manufacture of traction engines in 1877 with steam road rollers following in the 1890s as legislation bought increasing road development. A partially completed 10-ton roller stands nearest the camera with several traction engines behind.

Taken in the Southern Railway goods yard in 1906, this was a promotional photograph for Wallis & Steevens and James Moody rather than Moody's regular conveyance. The 5-ton steam wagon was then the latest development for Wallis & Steevens and this vehicle was photographed with a variety of loads as well as this slightly preposterous configuration. Moodys eventually bought a steam wagon in 1919.

Chapel Hill junction with Sherborne and Kingsclere Roads, *c.* 1900.

London Central Meat Co. Ltd, No. 26 Wote Street, *c.* 1910. Though pre-cooked frozen food was still a long way off, the transportation of frozen meat across the oceans began in the 1870s and the specialised distribution of such products as New Zealand's Canterbury lamb brought with it the first chains of retail butchers.

Above: Frederick Watson and his wife from Wote Street in their Léon Boliée 3hp Voiturette in 1898. Some debate surrounds who was Basingstoke's first motorcar owner, but when Evelyn Ellis and Frederick Simms passed through Basingstoke in their 4hp Panhard and Levassor at 11 a.m. on the 6 July 1895, driving from Micheldever to Datchet on the first ever long-distance journey by car in the UK, a new age had truly begun.

Left: Church Street, a watercolour by N.E. Edwards, *c.* 1900. Cattle in the street remained a familiar sight until the 1930s, with at least one anecdotal incident of a bull getting into a china shop.

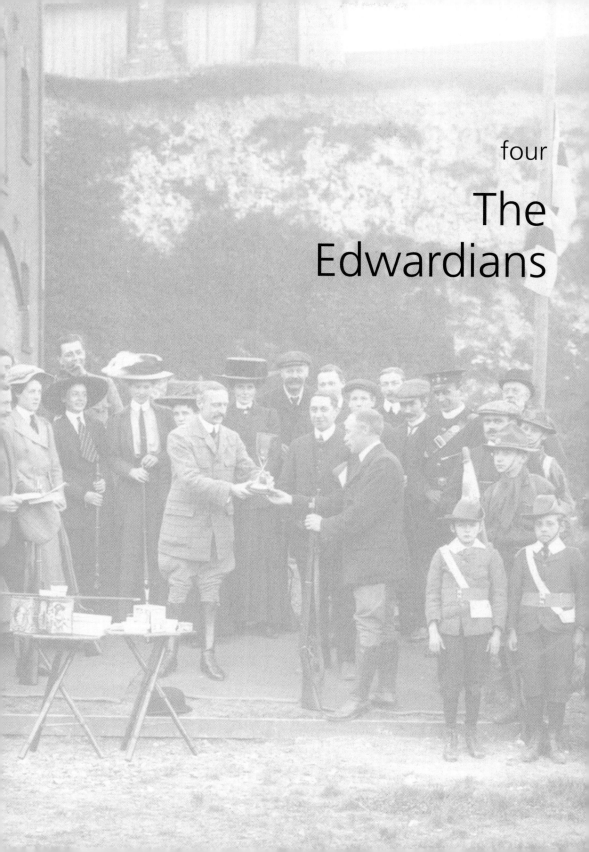

four

The Edwardians

Thornycrofts Steam Wagon Co. Ltd Worting Road, *c.* 1903. Work started in 1898 on what would become for many years Basingstoke's largest employer. Thornycrofts' lightweight, advanced designs were the antithesis of Wallis & Steevens products, but both shared the combination of reliability and sound engineering that allowed these companies to endure as others fell by the wayside.

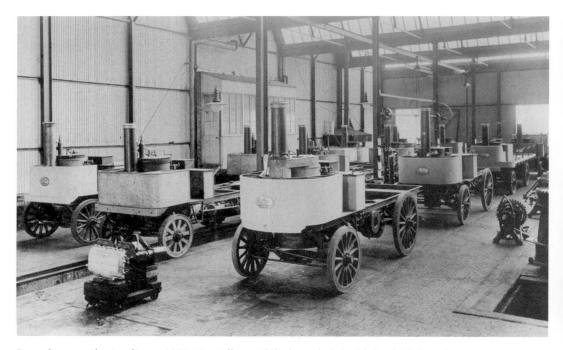

Steam lorry production line, *c.* 1899. War Office trials had concluded with Lord Kitchener's assessment that 'Thornycrofts are the best', and the company supplied the British Army in South Africa during the Boer War, the first contract in a long and successful association with the military. An example of one of these early lorries can be seen in the Milestones Museum.

John Wheeler's saddle makers shop, No. 60 Wote Street, dressed for the Coronation of Edward VII in 1902. According to directories, Wheeler was 'patentee of the celebrated adjustable ladies, gents and military riding saddles', and supplier to the Vine Hunt.

That year's celebrations took place on 9 August and included this parade, with the Volunteer Fire Brigade – equipped since 1891 with their more sophisticated steam pump – approaching down Station Hill. The buildings on the left house the clothing firm of Gerrish, Ames & Simpkins.

Perhaps earlier that same day, or preparing for the party afterwards, John May and Co.'s brewery put together this magnificent cortège. Lt-Col. John May was a very benevolent mayor, personally contributing the equivalent of £3,000 at today's values towards these Coronation celebrations and also making an identical donation on behalf of his brewery.

Known locally as 'The Colonel', he was born in Church Street and became mayor six times between 1883 and 1902. Here he's looking perhaps a little wary at the children's fancy dress ball in October 1902, another event he financed, held in the Drill Hall on Sarum Hill which he had paid for and which he'd had built, before presenting it to the town. George Willis wryly observed he was, 'a man who spent money freely in Basingstoke in order to obtain a knighthood, but he just evaded it'!

Church Square, *c.* 1906. The new Wesleyan Methodist chapel, opened in 1905, replaced a building on the same site that now stands in Cliddesden. The initial proposal was for a hideous gothic monstrosity to 'complement' St Michael's. As built, however, it was perhaps the greatest single architectural loss in the 1960s redevelopment. The design was heavily inspired by The Holy Trinity church in Sloane Street, London.

Bramblys Lane, *c.* 1900. Known as Bromlies in the sixteenth century, a streamlet of the Loddon used to flow across the track at the foot of this hill. Near there, when Penrith Road was being built, George Willis observed signs left by what may have been the very first humans to roam the Basingstoke area.

Wallis & Steevens 15-ton roller No. 7234, Southern Railway Goods Yard, 1911. By now reaching the height of their success, this mighty vehicle was one of the largest built by the company and was destined for Barcelona.

North Hants Ironworks Band, 1907. One of several brass bands in the town at the time, the man on the far right may be their band-leader Alf Lane but otherwise, sadly, we don't know the names of these fine-looking chaps.

The Market Place, 1902. The town's population was somewhere around 2,300 when Basingstoke's market was first recorded in the Domesday Book of 1086 and since 26 June 1214, a market has been held on a Wednesday. The Market Place was the site of the town's stocks and whipping post (used as recently as 1820), both were removed when the Market Place was enlarged in the 1830s.

Cliddesden Road junction with Fairfields Road, *c.* 1910. The development of reliable gas mantles around the turn of the century allowed smaller, brighter and more ornate street lamps like the one outside this sub-post office; it also delayed the introduction of electric lighting for some years.

CHURCH ST.

Above: Church Street, *c.* 1905. The quiet end of Church Street at rush hour. The car parked outside what was then the town clerk's office is an 8hp De Dion-Bouton. Relatively cheap – equivalent to about £8,500 today - and reliable, the De Dion was an important vehicle in convincing sceptical manufacturers that the internal combustion engine had a long-term future. Thornycrofts made their first petrol-engined prototype in 1902 with series production commencing the following year.

Left: Church Street, near the Market Place, *c.* 1905. Although the greenery below Cross Street now obscures this view, it was captured poetically in Diana Stanley's wonderful book about Basingstoke *Within Living Memory* published in 1967. Diana, who died in 1975, was probably Basingstoke's most famous artist. A former president of Basingstoke Art Club, she enjoyed commercial success as an illustrator of such well-known children's books as Mary Norton's *The Borrowers* and Barbara Euphan Todd's *Worzel Gummidge*. Her legacy of pastel illustrations and drawings of the town before its redevelopment can still be enjoyed in several of the town's libraries.

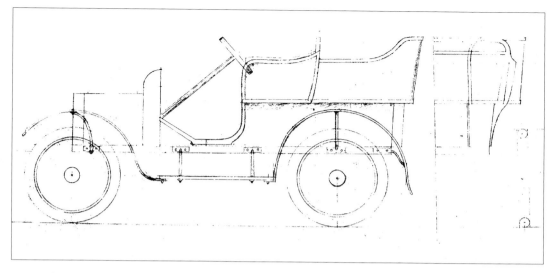

Above: Design for motor-car body by John Joice, Winchester Street, *c.* 1908. Many early car makers only manufactured the rolling chassis for their cars leaving the choice of bodywork to the customer. Joice were one of many carriage builders to exploit this short-lived market before car design and manufacture advanced.

Below: The Old Toll House, Hackwood Road, *c.* 1910. Mechanical threshing produced straw unsuitable for thatching, while houses built for thatch needed considerable expenditure to support heavier roofing material. Combined together these two factors quickly reduced picturesque charm to untenantable hovel and almost led to the extinction of Hampshire's thatched cottages. The ones along Hackwood Road were demolished in 1929, and the last within Basingstoke in South View in 1971.

P.J. Hopkin's Confectioners and Soda Fountain, London Street, 1910. Before the bottling of fizzy drinks was perfected, soda fountains enjoyed a brief popularity in the UK and a restored example from Church Crookham can be seen in Milestones Museum. An even more fleeting American import was the roller-skating craze – here advertised at the Corn Exchange, '4 Sessions Daily accompanied by Military Orchestration'. The Basingstoke rink opened in March 1910 and closed in May 1913.

Fry's chocolate – seen in the mouth-watering window display – was made by J.S. Fry & Sons in Bristol and Dr Joseph Fry, who began the company, trained as an apothecary and doctor in Basingstoke under Dr Henry Portsmouth in the 1740s, later marrying his daughter before returning to Bristol.

All Saints church, Southern Road, c. 1905. Opened in 1902, this little tin tabernacle catered temporarily for Christian worship in the expanding suburbs south of the town. It was built on a plot of land donated by the sisters of the then vicar of Basingstoke, Dr Cooper Smith, and when All Saints church proper was built, was moved and became the church hall. It still stands today although now timber clad and stripped of most of the charming details seen here.

The Plough, Hackwood Road, 25 April 1908. Opened in 1898. Despite the fact that May's were said to serve the best bitter in Basingstoke, The Plough struggled to compete with its rival The Lamb, only 100 yards further down the road, and closed in 1928.

Essex Road and Southend Road junction, 25 April 1908. The worst spring snowfalls on record hit north Hampshire on this day in 1908 when fourteen hours of continuous heavy snow left many roads virtually impassable. Typically, the sun shone the next day – which may have been when the photographer actually recorded these scenes – and by 29 April all the snow had melted.

Winchester Street from the Market Place, *c.* 1910. John May's benefaction during Victoria's Jubilee was commemorated by the burgesses with the lamppost seen here, installed in 1887. Then in 1903, again in appreciation, it was extended with an additional granite plinth decorated with four bronze plaques to celebrate the colonel's and his family's mayoralties.

Winchester Street, east, from New Street crossroads, *c.* 1904. Terry Hunt, who took this and many other photographs in this section, was one of Basingstoke's most prolific commercial photographers between about 1902 and 1939. Operating with a variety of half-plate cameras, he took hundreds of photographs of Basingstoke and its surrounding villages, which helped satisfy the booming postcard trade.

Wote Street, *c.* 1910. Shops have spread rapidly down the street since the 1860 photograph, which was taken slightly to the south of this one. Smith and Grippers grocery shop stands behind the lady with her bicycle on the right. A certain Mr Franklin who began work at this shop in 1875 was still working there happily in 1947 aged ninety-two.

Winchester Street, west, from New Street, *c.* 1910. Prominent in Winton Square is the library sign above Knowles' stationers. This was a circulating library where you could rent out books such as popular fiction. Although the Mechanics Institute operated a free technical library, Basingstoke's first free public lending library did not open until 1928, almost ten years after legislation had made provision of a free library service possible.

Kempshott House, *c.* 1910. Originally the seat of the Pinkes, this house was built around 1774 though subsequently much modified. George IV rented it while he was Prince of Wales, nominally as a hunting-lodge but mainly for illicit romps with uncourtly lady friends. Sir Guy Carlton, former Governor General of Quebec, was a famous eighteenth-century owner. During the twentieth century it passed through several hands declining rapidly before its demolition in 1972.

Worting Road, junction with Essex Road (right), *c.* 1910. The late Victorian expansion along Worting Road resulted in some splendid middle-class villas and fondly remembered working-class terraces further north in May Street and Lower Brook Street. Here a Fowler Road locomotive chuffs towards us with what looks like two trailer loads of timber.

Basingstoke Rifle Club, The Steam Dell, *c.* 1910. Far left: Mr Bird. On platform, Dr Macfarlane, Miss Cooper, Miss Simmonds, Mrs Prance and Mr F. Hillary presenting trophy. Far right: Mrs Yates, Mr Ray. A disused chalk pit behind the Little Almshouses on Reading Road became popularly known as 'The Steam Dell' after a steam seed mill and a terrace of houses – called Steam Mill Terrace – were built there in the 1860s. The rifle club met there regularly until 1914.

Basingstoke Station forecourt, London & South Western Railway, *c.* 1910. The station was greatly enlarged between 1898 and 1902 with a new goods yard opened off Chapel Street. In 1902 the first commercial passenger service began through-working from L&SWR to GWR lines and though still independently run, as far as the public were concerned, Basingstoke's two separate stations slowly began to blur into one.

The Grand Exchange Cinema, Wote Street, August 1913. Entrepreneur George Casey took over the lease for the Corn Exchange in July 1913 and opened it as a combined cinema and Vaudeville theatre. That same year the volunteer fire brigade moved out into a purpose-built station in Brook Street complete with the town's first motorised fire engine.

Basingstoke Conservative and Unionist Club Bowling Green, No. 47 Church Street, c. 1910. The club opened in 1909 in premises designed by architect W. Roland Howell, converted from existing houses on the site. The large building overshadowing the photograph is Smith Bros grain warehouse off Wote Street.

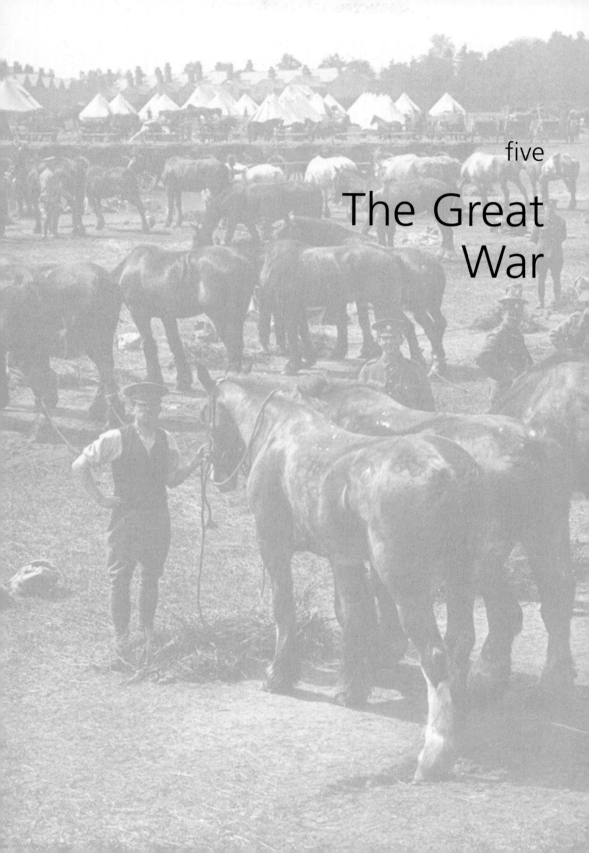

five

The Great
War

Sarum Hill, *c.* 1914. Basingstoke was no longer a quiet backwater, its population was now around 12,000 and despite complaints about 'wasting ratepayer's money', electric street lighting began to replace gas.

Winchester Street from the Market Place, *c.* 1914. Most of the year, attention had focussed upon home rule in Ireland, and when Britain declared war on Germany at midnight on 4 August 1914, it was almost with an air of nonchalance from the government. Shops in the town had to close early following the announcement as people began panic buying.

View west along Potter's Lane, August 1915. Things carried on much as normal at first; there were complaints in the paper about delivery boys speeding down Wote Street and Church Street without bells or brakes: 'endangering life and limb', and demands that ladies should be obliged to remove their hats in the cinema.

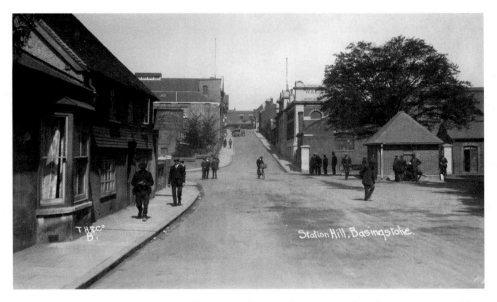

Wote Street, junction with Station Hill, *c.* 1914. The British Army was described as 'contemptibly small' by the Kaiser and by 1915, no single, able-bodied man could walk down the street without fear of being pestered about why he hadn't volunteered to serve his country. Special badges were produced for those on 'essential' war work though this scheme was eventually abandoned as it became impossible to define accurately what work was unessential.

Winchester Road, May 1915. Basingstoke became an important staging area for troop movements in the south. Lord Kitchener at Hackwood personally inspected this particular division before its departure for Gallipoli. The track from the Basingstoke and Alton light railway – in the background here – was lifted and shipped to France in 1916 to assist the war effort.

Charter Alley, 1915. Described by pilots as a 'bloody awful plane', this B.E.2 aircraft flipped after hitting a hedge during an emergency landing after running out of fuel; both plane and crew survived. In 1916 the same plane collided with another during training exercises and both pilots were killed.

Reading Road, *c.* 1916. Approximately 300 men who were born or who lived in Basingstoke were killed during the war, 234 of whom are recorded on the war memorial. Two local brothers, Alfred and Frederick Lush whose parents lived in East Oakley, died within three days of each other in September 1916.

Market Square, *c.* 1916. On the right in Winchester Street, the London, City and Midland Bank was built in 1915 and work also began on All Saints church, but life on the home front began to be affected as prices started to rise. Involuntary emancipation began in the workplace as women took jobs there were simply not enough men left to fill.

Holy Ghost Cemetery, 4 September 1915. Captain John Liddell of Sherfield Manor, Sherfield-on-Loddon, heroically returned his aircraft and navigator to Allied lines despite sustaining massive injuries himself and was awarded a Victoria Cross for his efforts. Sadly he died a month later from his wounds and was buried with full military honours.

The Market Place, c. 1916. Troops were regularly marched through the town on their way from Aldershot to Salisbury Plain and vice versa. These men are on their way to Salisbury and are receiving refreshment provided by staff from the Old Angel Café.

Women's Football Team, Thornycrofts' Football Ground, Worting Road, c. 1917. Thornycrofts' importance to the town and to the war effort became increasingly significant as the war went on. The plant expanded massively and by the end of the war employed over 1,500 people, over a third of whom were women. The men's football team were known locally as 'The Motor Boys'.

Women War Workers, Thornycrofts, 1916. As well as thousands of 'J' type lorries for the army, the plant supplied Stokes trench mortars and thousands of bomb and depth charge throwers. Total output during the four years of war exceeded that of all the preceding fifteen years.

'Girl gardeners', Schroeder's Nurseries, Cranbourne Lane, *c.* 1917. One of the less savoury aspects of the war was violent animosity shown towards anyone with a foreign sounding name. Gustav Schroeder, who was Danish and billed himself as 'Britain's largest Cucumber Grower', was one of several who found themselves having to defend their reputation through the local newspaper.

Land girl, *c.* 1918. Successful German naval blockades brought about a major food crisis, and in February 1917 the Women's Land Army was established to help with the acute shortage of farm labour. In comparison to women factory workers they were very poorly paid and their vital role in this conflict is often overlooked. (One of a series of photographs by Eric Guy, stationer of Winton Square)

Entertaining patients at the Red Cross Hospital, West Ham House, Worting Road, *c.* 1918. One of several temporary hospitals set up in the region to cater for convalescing soldiers. By the end of the war over 1,600 patients had passed through its doors.

Park Prewett Hospital Railway, 1917. Work on the asylum had restarted in 1913 only to be stopped once again by the war. The partially complete complex was opened as a temporary 150-bed military hospital in 1917. After completion of the asylum, the railway siding was used primarily to transport coal to the site and is not believed to have ever carried patients. The line closed in 1950.

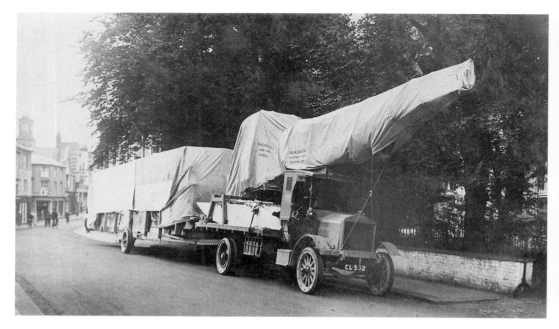

A Mann Egerton–built aircraft in transit, Winchester Road, c. 1918. Increased output, improved military tactics and the naval blockade of Germany gradually turned the tide in the war, but not before life on the home front became more difficult. A voluntary rationing scheme was introduced in 1917 but failed to make much effect and in 1918 compulsory rationing of sugar, meat, butter, cheese and margarine was introduced. Coal and petrol usage was also strictly controlled.

Women motorcyclists on a Douglas 2 3/4hp, Winchester Road, c. 1918. The war did not bring women equality or the vote; but for single, working-class women it introduced a much wider range of opportunities, gave them a voice in the workplace through trade union membership and sounded the death knell for domestic service.

On 16 November following the announcement of the armistice, official celebrations took place throughout the town culminating with the burning of an effigy of the Kaiser on Basingstoke Common. Canon Boustead proposed a war memorial immediately after the armistice, and debate on its nature included suggestions of a hall, an art gallery or even a 'museum' of war mementoes before the memorial park and monument were decided upon.

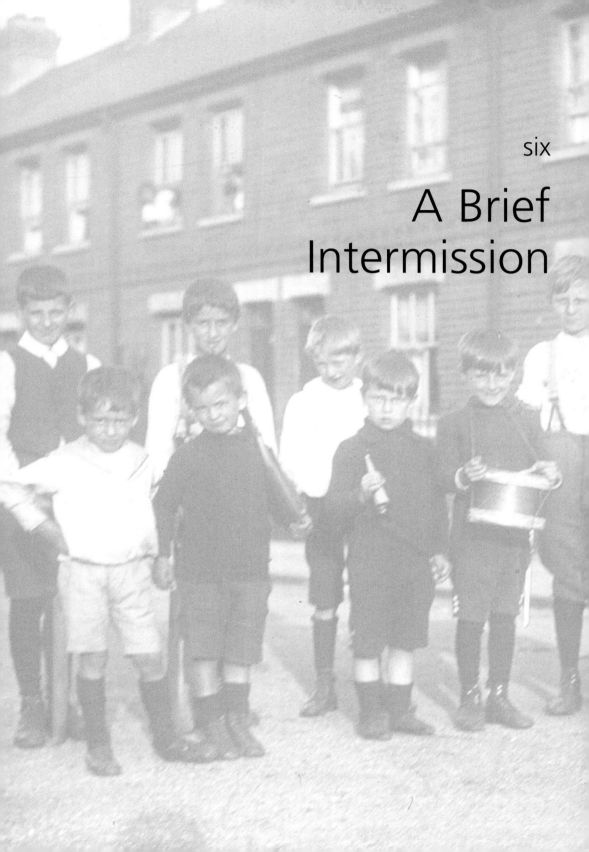

six

A Brief Intermission

H.M. The King inspecting Girl Guides, Laverstoke. 19

Laverstoke Lane, 10 April 1923. Visit by King Edward VII to Portals Mill. Portals had manufactured bank note paper for the Bank of England since 1727 and in the 1920s began manufacture for other countries as well. The King's visit to Portal's Overton and Laverstoke Mills was repeated forty years later by Queen Elizabeth.

Auction Pens, Vyne Road, 7 May 1923. Following their introduction in the 1870s by Hugh Raynbird, livestock auctions held near the station had quickly made redundant the annual livestock fairs of old whilst inadvertently allowing farmers to bypass the use of the corn exchange. Discussions after the war about building a new corn exchange nearer the station came to nothing.

George Street, *c.* 1920. The death of so many young men in the war did little to slow Britain's rapid population growth; the growth of Basingstoke's population was more than matched by the development of new housing and by 1921 there was an average of 4.4 people per house compared to 5.2 in 1891 despite a population increase of 55 per cent in the same period.

Hackwood Road, 1923. William Weaver built this wonderful little shop and tearoom in the garden of the Toll House cottage right next to the entrance to the park. Unfortunately it proved so successful that it was quickly redeveloped and incorporated into a much larger building when the cottage next door was demolished. The bay window beneath the awning is still recognisable today.

Water Polo Team, West Ham baths, *c.* 1925. Built for a grand total of £578 in 1906, the swimming baths probably represented the greatest value – pound for pound – of any of the town's civic amenities. Despite being open-air and particularly noted for its freezing cold water, it remained enormously popular until its enforced closure in 1966.

Church Street junction with Brook Street, *c.* 1925. The piecemeal development of the lower part of the town is perhaps shown to its worst here. This uncoordinated mix of industrial and humble architecture had plenty to interest individually, but as a whole got an unqualified thumbs-down by tourist guides and architectural critics.

Above: J Wiggins & Son, Grocers, Vyne Road, *c.* 1925. By the mid–1920s everyday motoring had become a lethal combination of poor driving skills, feeble brakes, narrow tyres, imprecise steering and dim lights. Almost every week the pages of *The Gazette* were filled with grim details of the often fatal outcome of relatively minor incidents. The introduction of the Highway Code in 1931, the driving test in 1934 and the gradual adoption of windscreen wipers from the late 1920s all helped to stem the tide.

Right: Mechanics Institute fountain, New Street, 1924. The fountain and front garden were sold to the council in 1925 for road widening.

Brook Street, 16 January 1926. Brook House is on the left. A severe cold snap in the middle of January brought deep snow to the south with 30cm being recorded in Farnborough on 16 January and a temperature of –16.7°C in Luton. Meteorologically the snow was not particularly significant, but it certainly made for some picturesque photographs.

All Saints church, 18 January 1926. The most architecturally important of all Basingstoke's churches, All Saints was designed by the architect Temple Moore and was his last major work. It has been described variously as 'dignified', 'noble' and as 'a work of art' and is without doubt one of the finest twentieth-century churches in the country.

Church Street, *c*. 1928. There were strikes at Thornycrofts in 1920 and at the railway and electricity works during the General Strike of 1926, but overall the town seems to have weathered the industrial unrest of that era with little disruption and only moderate unemployment – 8.3 per cent compared to 12.7 per cent nationally. Hot weather did cause a water shortage in 1929 though and there was a hosepipe ban.

Cranbourne Lane Nurseries, *c*. 1936. The detached glasshouses on the left are now the site of Cranbourne School. More would be added either side of Cranbourne Lane and on the far side of Winchester Road before the war as various companies combined their resources to form Basingstoke Joint Nurseries. In 1935 land was offered for an airport in this area but the council eventually decided against the idea.

Above: Thornycrofts' lorries leaving the factory for chassis testing, *c.* 1929. Thornycrofts were by now billing themselves as 'The leading exponents of economical road transport' and by 1930 the works along Worting Road had grown to cover more than 20 acres. The 1930s, however, bought their first downturn in business, some staff were laid off and output became more rationalised.

Above: Worting Post Office, 1932. Fortunately the only casualties in this incident were the pride of the Army driver and the hedge in front of the shop.

Right: Eastrop Lane, showing the 'dangerous humpback bridge' over the canal prior to road widening and development in the 1930s. Eastrop was merged with Basingstoke parish in 1932.

Opposite below: Brook Street, *c.* 1930. One of several photographs in a series by Terry Hunt that show Basingstoke fire brigade dealing with a mock 'incident' at the old Silk Mill for newsreel cameras. Unfortunately I have not been able to establish details of this event.

Above: The opening of the Basingstoke Trade Exhibition at the town hall by Lady Portal, April 1935. It featured stands by all the major companies in Basingstoke and included a full size working model of a Thornycroft engine. Over 1,000 people attended on the first day and almost 9,000 during the course of the exhibition.

Above: Reading Road, *c.* 1930. The Old House at Home pub in Bunnian Place is in the background. Though outwardly calm and peaceful, politically this was an unsettled time. Both William Joyce and Sir Oswald Mosley gave speeches in the town in the 1930s on behalf of the British Union of Fascists and were popularly well received.

Right: London Street – Hackwood Road Junction, *c.* 1930. An RAC patrolman was stationed permanently at this junction until 1939 to help control traffic.

Opposite below: Church Street, 1935. Sadly most of this row of jettied shops was demolished and redeveloped in 1937 leaving only the furthest standing, which eventually became the Army & Navy Stores before its demolition in the 1960s. Impossible to date accurately from photographs, the lack of close studding or angled timbers on the nearest suggests it may possibly have been pre-fifteenth century in date.

Above: Fred Smith's shop in Junction Road in 1930, on the corner with Station Hill and just a few yards from their first shop. The company began in Twyford in the 1880s and developed into one of the most important agricultural agencies in the south. Amongst other things they specialised in, were water supplies and well boring. Basingstoke was by now being promoted as, 'The commercial capital of North Hants' with rateable values 'amongst the lowest in the UK'. The population was nearing 14,000.

Left: Miss Harriet Costello MA, 1935. Taken on her retirement after twenty years as the head of Basingstoke High School for Girls. She was very highly regarded by both friends and colleagues and the school eventually adopted her name in 1972 when it became a comprehensive. Her retirement present from the school was a comfortable leather armchair.

Aston's Arcade, Church Street, September 1935. Opened in 1930, the fire at Aston's drapers broke out at 1.35 a.m. on 29 August. Despite the alarm being raised quickly, the entire premises were destroyed with the sole exception of one showcase of ladies underwear, heroically dragged to safety by the firemen.

Conservative Club, Church Street, decorated for George V's Silver Jubilee in 1935. Private motoring was still confined to a privileged few, but the town's narrow streets necessitated the building of a southern by-pass for through traffic in the 1930s.

Mount Pleasant Villas, Southern Road, decorated for the Coronation of George VI in 1937. This was the year that filming took place of the Will Hay comedy *Oh Mr Porter* on the remaining stump of the Basingstoke & Alton light railway. Born out of territorial rivalry between the GWR and SR, the railway had closed to passengers in 1932 after a colourfully brief but wholly unprofitable life.

Wote Street junction with Basing Road, *c.* 1936. The newly erected Waldorf Cinema stands behind Palethorpes' Royal Cambridge sausages on the left. According to *The Gazette*, the original intention was to name it the Troxy.

Hospital carnival float, 1938. Three carnivals were held pre-war to raise money for a new hospital planned for Cliddesden Road. This is Mrs D. Parham of Grove Road and her team with their winning entry in the hand-pushed vehicles category. *Gladstone* was the locomotive in *Oh Mr Porter* and I think Mrs Parham is the Will Hay look-alike on the right.

Levelling the site for Eli Lilly's near Kingsclere Road, 1938. Planning and development became more official and proactive in the 1920s with the formation of the Basingstoke & District Joint Town Planning Scheme and the Basingstoke Development Committee. This work quickly bore fruit attracting companies like Eli Lilly's, Auto Tyre Services and Kelvin, Bottomley & Baird along with the building of over 600 new council houses around the town between 1920 and 1938.

London Street, 1938. Britain failed to act as Germany built up its military forces in the early 1930s. The British public felt that to act against German aggression would risk war and consequently few politicians spoke out against appeasement. 'We have a moral obligation to be friends with Germany' as Basingstoke's MP put it shortly before Czechoslovakia was invaded.

Church Street peace parade, 8 July 1939. Youth clubs from the Basingstoke area march to Castle Field for a sports day and community singing. By now war was seen as inevitable and prayer perhaps the only hope. In the months before war was declared, the blackout and air-raid skills were practiced and almost 1,000 evacuees arrived in the town on 1 September. War was declared at 11.15 a.m. on 3 September 1939.

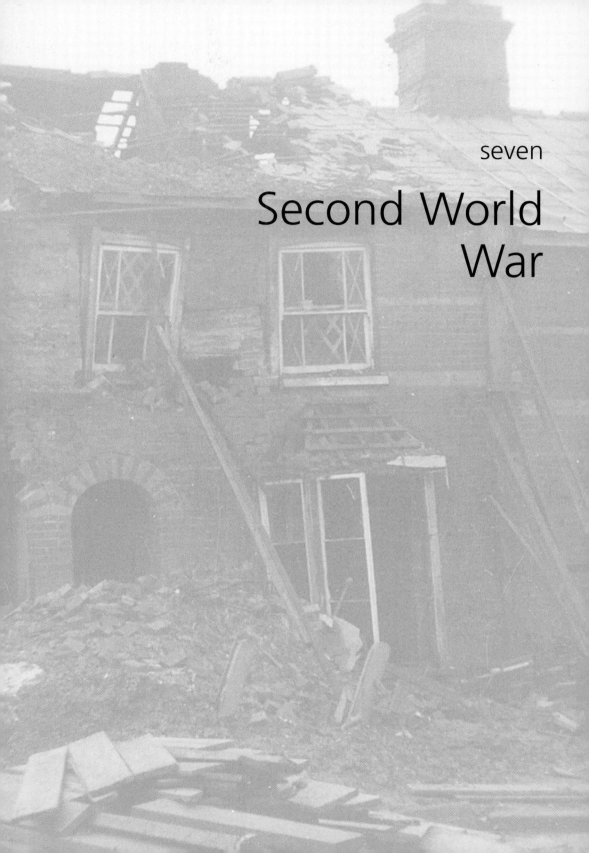

seven

Second World War

The Lilly Building camouflaged in maroon and brown, taken from the roof of Thornycroft, c. 1939. In the months before the declaration, official buildings were protected with sandbags and air-raid trenches; school buildings got nothing which caused some disquiet. Blackout regulations extended as far as the partial masking out of rear reflectors on bicycles.

Thornycroft's factory, c. 1939. The camouflage may look ineffective, but while bombs fell in the town and the surrounding countryside, Thornycroft was never hit. Staff protection was well catered for with twenty-four shelters around the site, capable of holding up to 1,400 people.

Goldings, London Road, *c.* 1939. In the town there were large shelters at the junction of Basing Road and Wote Street, in the gardens of London Street Almshouses and in the cellars of the George, the Grapes and the Victoria. The Savoy Cinema opened on 23 October 1939 in Wote Street, and in May 1940 the Germans reached the coast of France.

Above, left and right: Church Street. At 5.15 p.m. on 16 August 1940, the air-raid siren sounded as enemy aircraft approached. Shortly afterwards bombs exploded near the church and in Burgess Road. Ten people were killed and a number seriously injured. The railway line was also hit.

Church Square, August 1940. Thankfully, the scale of death and destruction of 16 August was never repeated, though four others died in later bombing attacks and five soldiers were killed dealing with an unexploded bomb just outside the town.

Solby's Road, 9 November 1940. The same day that Neville Chamberlain – the former prime minister who had hoped to bring 'Peace in our time' – died from cancer at nearby Heckfield.

Salute the Soldier Parade, Market Place, June 1944. A scandal developed in 1940 involving the then Viscount Lymington, self-elected Home Guard Platoon Commander for nearby Cliddesden, Dummer, Ellisfield and Farleigh. Asked to step down from his post as a suspected fifth columnist, he refused and was forcibly removed by the Hampshire Commander. Nothing was ever substantiated and he continued to serve loyally afterwards as a private.

Salute the Soldier Parade, Wote Street, June 1944. Each year during the conflict a differently themed week was held to help finance the war by borrowing money from the public through national savings campaigns. The 1944 campaign raised £620,813 in the town. Three flying bombs fell near the town in 1944. The closest, by the swimming baths, caused minor damage to almost 300 homes although amazingly no one was hurt.

May Street, 1945. It was clear by the winter of 1944 that the long war was finally coming to an end. The blackout was relaxed in September and replaced with the 'dim-out' and the home guard stood down in December. George Formby had been in the town in 1944 filming *He Snoops to Conquer*, and the film was given its Basingstoke premiere in March 1945.

Francis Road, 1945. Celebrations after VE-Day were unrestrained. Church bells were rung, there was dancing in the streets and Eli Lilly's was floodlit even though it was still camouflaged. Dozens of street parties were held around the town culminating with a party for over 2,000 children in the War Memorial Park.

eight

Post-War Redevelopment

E.C. White's timber yard. The main sawmill, facing Wote Street, 1946. Whites' timber yard, established in 1792 and Basingstoke's last direct link with the canal, remained in operation on what was the southern part of the canal wharf until shortly after the death of Robert White in 1946. The site was auctioned off in October that year and E.C. Whites was amalgamated with The Basingstoke Timber Co. in Brook Street. The wharf site was cleared for a new bus station.

E.C. Whites' timber yard, Basingstoke Wharf, view north-east – the lorry in the distance is parked in what had been the canal basin. The canal wharf had been in-filled in the 1920s and the north-west corner of the site levelled for a new cattle market. The market saw little use and that corner was again cleared; later to be used for The Waldorf Cinema in 1935 along Wote Street and the war-time British Restaurant on the corner of Reading Road.

Worting Road, near the junction with Buckskin Lane, *c.* 1948. The war had brought more social change. Despite the enforced restrictions, food controls and full employment meant the lower classes were better fed and better paid than ever before. Gradually during the war a vision of a socially balanced 'new Britain' emerged with a social insurance scheme, the National Health Service and a 'new deal' in housing and education. The population had continued to rise steadily and in the early post-war years private transport was artificially restricted by the devaluation of the pound and petrol rationing.

Acton's Almshouses, Flaxfield Road, *c.* 1952. Bequeathed to the poor around 1690 by James Acton, these houses had been restored in 1890 but were neglected in the 1940s after the occupants were re-housed. It was hoped, as they adjoined the site of the library and museum, that they could be preserved as a cottage museum, but costs were felt to be prohibitive and they were demolished in 1953 and replaced by a small garage.

Above: London Street, 1948. Thornycrofts celebrated '50 years of Progress' in the town in 1948 by making a promotional film including their pioneer steam wagon of 1896. In August 1946 a talk was given by the North East Hants planning officer where a specific proposal to build 11,500 new houses in Basingstoke to house London overspill was first publicised.

Left: Trackbed of Basingstoke and Alton light railway, beside the Thornycrofts works, 1966. Since the 1920s, there had been a gradual shift in housing development from small schemes involving individual private patrons, to much larger developments by commercial groups or local authorities.

In response to this change and, with increasing costs of labour and traditional building materials as a percentage of overall building costs, the trend of post-war development throughout the country became one of large-scale developments using fewer skilled workers with much less attention paid to individuality or to intricate architectural detail. Aesthetics became subjugated by functionality and cost.

The Reformer's Tree, Reading Road, 1963. Without any assistance from the London overspill, Basingstoke's population had leapt by over 50 per cent between 1951 and 1961 – nine times the national average – and had reached 25,940. In this same period, car ownership by household had more than doubled from 14 per cent to around 30 per cent and was continuing to grow at an even faster rate.

Vermont Snack Bar, Reading Road, from the roof of Jackson's Garage, *c.* 1964. Many were attracted to the area by employment at the new Atomic Weapons Research Establishment at Aldermaston for which housing was built at Oakridge. Others simply by the availability of new housing or by employment prospects at large companies like Lansing Bagnall and Van Moppes.

View south from above the station with Station Hill and Wote Street to the left, 1962. In October 1961 it was officially announced that under an agreement between London County Council, Hampshire County Council and Basingstoke Borough Council, a plan would be drawn up to redevelop the town and build 11,500 new homes by 1976 to house part of London's overspill.

May Street, eastern end, 1963. A number of Parliamentary Acts were passed after the war that made the compulsory purchase of private land by government bodies relatively straightforward. Though not unchallengeable, they were until very recently unlikely to be overturned without expensive legal representation. The 'vision' for the town was to be a bold and bright clean sweep.

Brook Terrace, with the Cricketer's public house in the distance, 1963. The new town map and provisional development plan was published in August 1962 and showed clearly the full magnitude of the proposals. The only allusion to any preservation of Basingstoke's heritage in the plan was the sentence, 'There are six scheduled ancient monuments in the area of the Town Map, and every effort will be made to leave these undisturbed by development'. These were Winklebury Camp, The Holy Ghost chapel, Pyotts Hill entrenchments, Oliver's Battery, Basing House and the tithe barn in Old Basing. (Both pictures on this page were taken by F.T. Adnams)

Little Almshouses, Reading Road, 1966. Built in 1829 to replace others demolished in Chapel Street to accommodate the railway. Eight-page supplements were published in both local papers, and a public exhibition of the development proposals was given at the town hall in August 1962 including a model of the proposed new town centre. From all this publicity and the estimated 15,000 people who attended the exhibition over seven weeks, there were 273 objections.

The Victory Inn, Victory Square, Brook Street, 1963. With Top Not ladies' hairdressers on right. The relative lack of protest, challenge or dissent was surprising. As John Arlott, Basingstoke's famous writer and cricket commentator put it at the time 'Alas! Poor Basingstoke, no one seems to mind very much'. The accelerated population growth between 1951 and 1961 possibly helped to dilute and divide any major public opposition and the biggest protests came from individual traders, but even here there was insufficient support for any major fight against the plan. (Taken by FT Adnams)

Winchester Street, August 1966. The following series of photographs by Eric Lane shows a typical Saturday afternoon in the town shortly before redevelopment work began.

Above, left and right: New Street and Winchester Road junction, August 1966. A statutory public enquiry began in 1963, but less than half of the initial objections were pursued with sufficient vigour to be heard during its course. The golden vision of opportunity and improvement intimated by the plan appears to have been widely accepted. The town's Chamber of Commerce dropped plans to fight the changes due to lack of support.

Left: Winchester Street, August 1966. What does not seem to have been fully comprehended at this time was how long and how disruptive the transformation would be and also just how vague some of the proposals were. The redevelopment would change the entire nature of the town.

Above, left and right: Market Place, August 1966. Other factors that could not be anticipated in 1963 were that the transformation would be blighted throughout by shoddy workmanship, insensitivity, rampant inflation and a national backdrop of growing industrial and social unrest.

Right: London Street, August 1966. In 1964, after the enquiry had finished but before any work had started, the provisional nature of the plan became apparent when its dramatic headline-grabbing centrepiece, the raised shopping centre on a platform across the Loddon valley – possibly a major factor in winning the initial public approval for the overall scheme – was replaced by a much more prosaic design.

London Street, August 1966. London Street and Winchester Street were not only the town's main shopping streets until the redevelopment, but also one of the principal traffic routes through the town. This was a major factor in determining that the highest priority for the design should be the total separation of road traffic and pedestrians.

Nos 47/49 Church Street, 1966. Army and Navy Stores. Inadequate financial compensation and protracted settlements soured initial progress. These were calculated on the basis of what the market value of a freehold property might be without the redevelopment; it generally offered only leasehold replacements and made no provision for how the redevelopment in itself would substantially increase the cost of renting a substitute in the new centre.

View west along Potter's Lane, 1963. Difficult national economic conditions also delayed the start of building work and things went downhill from that point. The main building contractor got into financial difficulties, eventually going into liquidation and the increasingly complex interdependence between finance and return that was funding the development stilted progress so that further compromises became necessary. (Taken by P. & U. Jeffree)

Above: No. 26 Church Street, 1966 John Hugh's, outfitters opposite Cross Street junction. The wholesale demolition of the old town centre was a very bleak time and perhaps the nadir was reached in March 1967 with the suicide of pensioner John Isley from Winklebury who in a peak of depression drowned himself in a water tank in his garden following protracted delays in concluding the compulsory purchase and compensation process for his home. Such incidents drove an increasingly bitter wedge between the 'old Basingstoke' public and the developers.

Left: No. 24 Church Street, 1966. George Tibbitts, furniture dealer. Terry Hunt's photographic studio was on the top floor of the central building, above what was then Kemp's drapery shop.

Right: No. 18 Church Street, 1966. Tunbridge Jones, Basingstoke Mineral Water Co. Some proposed developments were abandoned only after the land had been compulsorily purchased and the sites cleared. A seven-storey hotel in New Street, a major civic centre between Cross Street and Church Square and what was described as an eleven-story skyscraper for the Berg estate, were amongst the failed plans.

Below: Church Street, 1966. Harold Hamblin's garage alongside the memorial gardens. In 1964 it was agreed that a new market place near to the bus station should replace the old one in front of the town hall. After it was built and was running successfully, it became clear that the cost and effort required to obtain the necessary Act of Parliament to allow the official closure of the old market was more trouble than it was worth and so for a number of years Basingstoke became a town with two separate markets and market places.

Nos 15 and 17 Cross Street, 1966. From left to right: Barnes & Avis, music shop, Delahay, ladies' outfitters. The new market place – imaginatively named New Market Square – was the first part of the new shopping centre to be built. Twenty-three small shop units surrounding the open-air Market Place on three sides. Displaced independent traders whose premises were demolished in the old town were given first choice of these new leasehold premises.

Rear view of Bedford House, 1966. Bedford House was one of a number of buildings provisionally Grade II Listed that were demolished in the redevelopment. Morris Minor Travellers proved to be somewhat easier to save.

View west toward the rear of the Methodist church, with Powell's builders' yard in the foreground, 1966. The last church service took place in October 1965.

Abandoned glasshouses behind the Methodist church and backing on to Bedford Place, 1966. Local caravan site and riding school owner Alfie Cole achieved national headlines with a carefully constructed media campaign conducted in partnership with ex–Fleet Street journalist Charles Hemsley against compulsory purchase. Riding to No. 10 Downing Street in a pony and trap to hand in a petition for better compensation to Harold Wilson in 1966, he followed this with a variety of stunts, culminating with the dumping of lorry loads of earth and rubble at several major junctions around the town, causing traffic chaos.

No. 52 Church Street, 1966. Samuel Nutt's stationers. Alfie's campaign won much public support though whether it was despite his campaign or because of it that the compensation he ultimately received was significantly increased is more debatable. Happily it allowed him to fulfil his dream by building what was then Britain's biggest indoor riding stadium near Micheldever.

Nos 17 and 19 Wote Street, 1966. From left to right: H.J. Aylward's, photographers, Priddy & Sons, fruiterers. Though yet to be fully completed, phase one of the shopping centre was officially opened in November 1968 and enormous crowds flocked in. Modern supermarkets and easy parking had come to Basingstoke.

No. 23a Wote Street, 1966. Tigwell & Stevens, builders, situated in the 1883 post office building erected by one of their founders. Perhaps surprisingly, given the emphasis on road transport in the development plan, aspects of the Ringways construction were cut back drastically. Much of the road would remain single carriageway for years and the overpasses carefully planned on all the major roundabouts remain unbuilt to this day.

Left: Nos 46a and 46b Wote Street, 1966. From left to right: Swift, dry cleaners, Decor, decorating materials. Amongst the more significant gains for the community was the new hospital, built in the grounds of Park Prewett, the first stage opened in October 1969 finally fulfilling the aspirations of the pre-war carnivals and relieving the majority of patients the ordeal of having to make long and tortuous trips to Winchester.

Below: View south along Wote Street with Saturday shoppers, 1966.

Nos 55 to 58 Wote Street, 1964. From left to right: F. Hedges, fruiterers, Tree & Co., newsagents, Fullers, café & confectioners. Amongst the losses was the premature closure of West Ham swimming baths, apparently forced upon the public and the borough council once the Ringway West surrounded the site in 1971. The road opened without ceremony but the volume of traffic using it meant that it was no longer safe to walk across the road to get to the public baths. With no underpass or other means of access forthcoming, the pool quickly closed through lack of use.

No. 44a Wote Street, 1966. Basingstoke Camera & Hi-fi Centre. The fact that the Sports Centre with its heated swimming pool had opened the year before was irrelevant to people who had enjoyed the facility at West Ham for most of their lives. Whether by accident or due to political stage management, what the public saw was that instead of a gala farewell to a much-loved facility, their wishes had been simply kicked aside. As the old pool slowly lay neglected, gathering a thick film of green algae, so rose the bitter resentment of town folk who saw this as yet another example of those in power riding roughshod over the people.

View north along Wote Street, 1967. As work on the new shopping centre neared completion, construction of a new road to by-pass London Street and Winchester Street was announced. Pound Road, as it was provisionally named, cut through the properties between Southern Road and the old high street, providing service access to the shops whilst at the same time allowing London Street and Winchester Street to be pedestrianised.

No. 63 Wote Street, 1966. The Savoy Cinema. When built in 1972, the name of Pound Road was dropped, as were plans for a multi-storey car park between Southern Road and the town. This left the area pretty much as we see it today, with the new, New Road around the town linking directly between the old, New Road and what remains of New Street.

Removal of the pediment from Queen Anne House, Church Street, 1966. By 1971, the population had leapt to 53,000 and despite all the chalk, upheaval and setbacks, phase one of the shopping centre had been completed, schools and houses had gone up and new companies were moving in. A contingency written into the plan at an early stage meant phase two, the link-up between the shopping centre and the railway station, could and would be postponed until the national economic climate was more favourable.

Reformer's Tree, 1967. The celebrated Hornbeam tree was chopped down later that year in what was undoubtedly the greatest reformation it ever bore witness to. (Taken by Mary Felgate)

Left: View south along Church Street, 1970. Whatever else the town centre redevelopment may have bought, it certainly did nothing to address any of the aesthetic criticisms of Basingstoke's past. The brutal clash of the old and new was apparent to all. Architectural pleasures were even more elusive than before and for the wistful traveller exploring the county's finer points, Basingstoke remained as it was portrayed in *Highways and Byways in Hampshire in 1908,* 'A town that may be hurried through'.

Below: New Market Square, September 1966. In broad terms the redevelopment scheme was a success – on paper Basingstoke was a better place. In detail and conduction it was poor, compromised throughout by inadequate financing and an apparent laissez-faire attitude by the developers to the public. Crime rates rose disproportionately and even the scheme's most passionate supporters were forced to conclude that this had not been a happy period.

Station Yard, December 1972. Phase two of the town centre development finally took place between 1978 and 1981. While Basingstoke remained a place that many people found hard to like, it proved a commercial magnet. Shops and companies came and went but the town as a whole prospered and throughout the 1980s Basingstoke had some of the highest rates of pay and lowest unemployment figures in the country.

Hackwood Road, July 1975. Broadly speaking this trend has continued and with steps taken to augment the town's social activity with the opening of the Anvil and the introduction of ice-skating, ten-pin bowling and other facilities at West Ham Leisure Park, many aspects have improved significantly. The rebuilding of some of the shopping centre in the Festival Place scheme opened in 2002 has removed a few of the worst eyesores and added much improved leisure facilities to the town's heart. Has Basingstoke now reached its newspaper's objective of being a place to be proud of? Only you can decide.

Other local titles published by Tempus

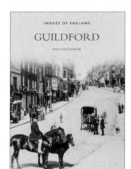

Around Woking

LYNDON DAVIES

This fascinating volume of old images traces some of the developments in Woking during the 1920s and early 1930s. Drawn from the archive of Woking photographer Sidney Francis, this collection of over 200 photographs, many never before published, highlights some of the important events that have occurred in the town during this time, including rare views of Woking Football Club, officials at Brookwood cemetery and visitors to Woking Mosque.

978 07524 3230 4

Haunted Winchester

MATTHEW FELDWICK

Drawing on historical and contemporary sources Haunted Winchester contains a chilling range of ghostly accounts. This selection includes tales of spectral monks at Winchester Cathedral and phantom horses in the Cathedral Close, as well as stories of the Eclipse Inn where Dame Alice Lisle, condemned by Judge Jefferies, still walks. This phenomenal gathering of ghostly goings-on is bound to captivate anyone interested in the supernatural history of the area.

978 07524 3846 7

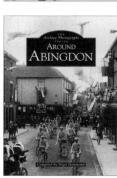

Guildford

PHILIP HUTCHINSON

Guildford still retains much of its 'Olde Worlde' charm into the twenty-first century; it is what makes it such a popular place for tourists from all over the world who come and take photographs of the Guildhall, the Castle and the picturesque River Wey. Most of the images in this book are from Philip Hutchinson's personal collection and are appearing here in print for the first time.

978 07524 4203 7

Around Abingdon

NIGEL HAMMOND

This intriguing collection of over 200 old photographs of Abingdon shows life in the town and surrounding villages over a period of more than one hundred years. The photographs include examples from the Victorian camera of the prolific Henry Taunt, pictures from Morland's Brewery, Abingdon School and a variety of social and working life recorded by amateur and professional photographers over the years.

0 7524 0392 3

If you are interested in purchasing other books published by Tempus, or in case you have difficulty finding any Tempus books in your local bookshop, you can also place orders directly through our website

www.tempus-publishing.com